History's Fearless Fighters

SAMURAI

Rupert
Matthews

Gareth Stevens
PUBLISHING

Please visit our website, **www.garethstevens.com**.
For a free color catalog of all our high-quality books, call toll free 1-800-542-2595 or fax 1-877-542-2596

Library of Congress Cataloging-in-Publication Data

Matthews, Rupert.
Samurai / by Rupert Matthews.
p. cm. — (History's fearless fighters)
Includes index.
ISBN 978-1-4824-3177-3 (pbk.)
ISBN 978-1-4824-3180-3 (6 pack)
ISBN 978-1-4824-3178-0 (library binding)
1. Samurai — Juvenile literature. I. Matthews, Rupert. II. Title.
DS827.S3 M38 2016
355.00952—d23

First Edition

Published in 2016 by
Gareth Stevens Publishing
111 East 14th Street, Suite 349
New York, NY 10003

© Alix Wood Books

Produced for Gareth Stevens by Alix Wood Books
Designed by Alix Wood
Editor: Eloise Macgregor

Photo credits:
Cover © Blend Images/Alamy, 1 © Metropolitan Museum of Art/Shutterstock; 3, 4, 5, 6, 8, 9, 11, 12, 14, 15, 18, 21, 22, 23, 37, 39 top, 41 top © Shutterstock; 10 © Los Angeles County Museum of Art; 16 bottom © Fukuoka Irina/Shutterstock.com ; 17 © Samuraiantiqueworld; remaining images are in the public domain

Printed in the United States of America
CPSIA compliance information: Batch #CS15GS: For further information contact Gareth Stevens, New York, New York at 1-800-542-2595.

Contents

The samurai finishes eating his lucky shellfish and hands the porcelain dish to his servant. He glances up at the flag that flutters over the heads of his unit, then draws his razor-sharp sword. The commander of the samurai raises his fan and waves it left, right, and then straight ahead. A huge cheer goes up. The samurai charge toward their enemy.

The samurai were professional warriors who dominated Japanese society for nearly a thousand years. A samurai could legally kill anyone who did not show the proper level of respect!

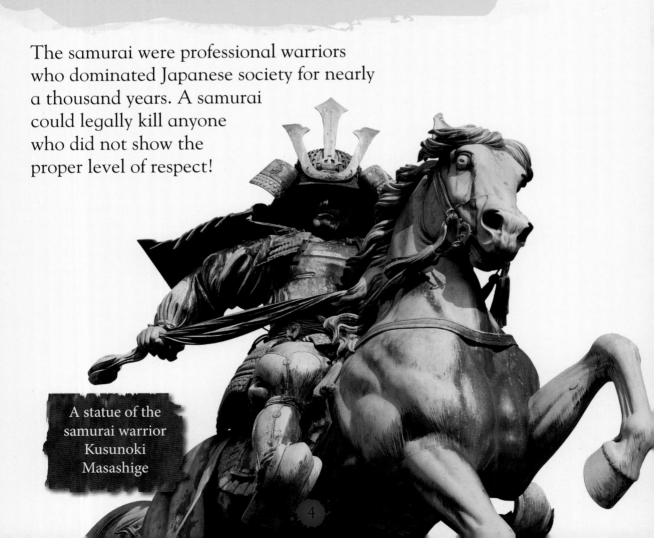

A statue of the samurai warrior Kusunoki Masashige

4

Samurai trained hard to become highly skilled with a variety of weapons, but it was the long sword that was always the most popular and honorable weapon. The swords of a samurai were highly valued family heirlooms that would be used by generations of the same family.

Samurai sword and sheath

A code of honor, called **bushido**, controlled nearly every aspect of samurai life. A samurai would rather die than break this code. Many killed themselves after accidentally breaking the code. Devotion to a lord was central to bushido, but bushido also demanded honesty, calmness, **piety**, and wisdom.

SAMURAI CULTURE

The samurai were **abolished** in 1878 as Japan wanted to modernize its society and culture. However, the **descendants** of the samurai still dominated Japan's government and armed forces for generations. Even today the culture and lifestyle of the samurai are strong influences on modern Japan.

The Changing Face of Samurai

O ver the course of about 1,300 years the role, status, and activities of the samurai changed. At different periods they could include very different types of men doing very different jobs. What they all had in common was the name of samurai.

In AD 702, Monmu, the 42nd Emperor of Japan, issued *The Code of Taiho*, which reformed the government. It ranked government officials into 12 classes, of which the lowest six were grouped together as "saburai." This word meant "a person who serves a nobleman," and covered all government officials who did day-to-day work.

The word "saburai" gradually changed to "samurai." A samurai was expected to serve a nobleman.

In about AD 850 Emperor Kanmu abolished the central army. He gave noblemen the job of enforcing law and order in their local areas. The emperor would call on the noblemen's armed supporters if he ever needed an army. These warriors adopted the title of samurai as they served the nobles. Over the next 200 years the samurai became a large, highly skilled force.

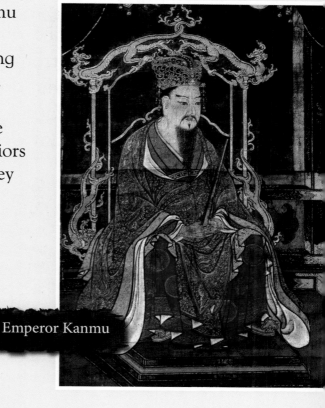

Emperor Kanmu

POWER AND STATUS

As the samurai grew in prestige they began to own land as well as serve as soldiers. They slowly replaced the nobles as the most important group in society. As this happened the samurai clans began to exclude others. A talented farmer's son could not become a samurai as he once could. By 1500 only the children of samurai could train to become samurai.

In the 1160s a nobleman named Taira no Kiyomori used his samurai to make himself ruler of Japan. The actual emperor at the time became a mere figurehead with little power.

When wars in Japan ended under the rule of the Tokugawa dynasty, the samurai became government officials, as well as nobles and warriors. They continued training as soldiers, but also gained other skills and talents.

Training to Be Samurai

A boy who wanted to become a samurai had to start early. Formal training began at the age of five, but even before that date a boy would be expected to go with his father to training sessions, sit quietly, and watch what went on.

Wealthy Boys

Boys from rich families were sent to one of the famous Samurai Academies. The boys lived in the academy for most of the year, returning to their families for important events. They learned about literature, religion, and honor as well as how to use their weapons and about battle tactics.

Poor Boys

Less wealthy families trained their boys at home. Not every father could train his son in all the skills of the samurai. Boys might be sent to live with a family friend for some months to learn one particular skill. Some samurai lords would pay for poorer boys to go to an academy if they passed certain tests.

In the winter months, boys training to be samurai were ordered to sit naked in the snow for hours at a time in order to toughen their bodies! They were also sent on runs in the snow, again naked, and made to wade through frozen rivers.

Boys began training with wooden weapons, reduced in size to match their height. At about age 9 boys began using blunt metal weapons, then moved on to sharp weapons at age 13. Blunt weapons were used when practicing against a fellow samurai. Sharp weapons were used when facing dummies, dogs, or slaves.

There was no set age when a samurai was considered ready to go into battle. Whenever the master samurai thought his pupil was ready, the boy was sent to join the men. A samurai was expected to continue training all his life.

The sport of kendo comes from a samurai training method and uses a bamboo sword.

That's Fearless!

One master samurai carried a wooden stick with him. He would lash out at his pupils at any time of day or night, until they learned to be on their guard at all times.

Tea and Poetry

The young samurai aimed to be good at the arts as well as at fighting. Some painted, others wrote stories, but poetry was most highly regarded. Samurai who wrote elegant poetry were as valued as those who fought well.

From about AD 850 onward the role of the samurai brought them into contact with the Imperial Court. Rather than appear as ignorant killers, the samurai began to learn about the arts and culture favored by the emperors. By about 1100 all samurai were taught to read and write, and to appreciate good quality literature.

Taira no Tadanori
about to sleep
under a cherry tree

POET WARRIOR

The 12th century samurai Taira no Tadanori was a famed poet. After he was killed in battle, this poem was found tucked into his arrow quiver:

Were I, still traveling as night falls,
to make a sheltering tree my inn,
then would my host tonight
be the blossoms themselves?

When Tadanori's friend Heike Monogatari heard of his death he composed an epitaph:

Friends and foes alike wet their sleeves with tears and said,
What a pity! Tadanori was a great general,
Preeminent in the arts of both sword and poetry.

BUNBO RYODO

The samurai believed in **bunbo ryodo** which means "the pen and the sword in one accord." If you called a samurai "**uruwashii**," which means "master of literature and fighting," that would be seen as a great compliment.

One of the arts a samurai was expected to excel in was the "Way of Tea." This **ceremonial** meal was served to guests. The rituals surrounding the making, serving, and drinking of tea varied depending on the time of year and time of day. The meal was judged by how correctly the rules were followed, the elegance of the movements, and the quality of the clothing, bowls, kettles, flowers, and other items used. The ceremony might take up to four hours!

The design of stone gardens was also an essential skill. The placing of rocks and gravel was intended to symbolize the inner meanings of natural landscapes. They were usually designed to be seen from one spot, where the samurai would sit and think.

The samurai also learned how to paint landscape pictures using black ink and brushes. Different shades were made by varying the thickness of the ink, the type of brush and the background material. Once a stroke had been made it could not be changed.

Becoming Ronin

Most samurai had a lord who provided them with land and money. The status of a samurai depended on the status of his lord, too. Samurai who did not have a lord were known as "ronin."

Few samurai chose to become ronin as they would have a lower status than if they had a lord. A samurai could become ronin if his lord died or punished him by throwing him out. Once trained, it would be a dishonor to stop being a samurai, so most ronin worked as warriors. Merchants hired ronin as bodyguards, or to escort valuable cargo through dangerous areas. Some lords would hire ronin for a short time in return for payment. A small number of ronin gave up fighting and became artists or monks.

The **kabukimono** were ronin who had taken to a life of crime. They were proud to be samurai, but robbed non-samurai. They were rude and violent, but were often tolerated by other samurai as long as they did no harm to samurai families. The kabukimono often wore outrageous costumes and wore red sword scabbards.

THE 47 RONIN

Samurai lord Asano Naganori was tricked by the court official Kira Yoshinaka into breaking a court rule. He was sentenced to death. His 47 samurai followers became ronin. Led by Oishi the 47 ronin wanted to avenge their lord, but Kira was guarded night and day. The ronin separated to become monks, artists, or bodyguards but kept in touch. After two years Oishi heard that Kira was staying at a **rural** house with only 50 guards. The 47 ronin fought their way into the house and killed Kira. Kira's head was placed on Asano's grave, along with prayers. The 47 ronin then calmly waited to be arrested. They were allowed to commit suicide like samurai rather than be executed like criminals. The youngest was allowed to live. The ronin were buried beside their lord. The story has often been made into movies and television series.

A woodblock print of the 47 ronin attacking Kira's house

Samurai Swords

Samurai swords have a reputation for sharpness, strength, and **durability**. The Japanese swordsmiths used great skill in making the swords. The fighting abilities of the samurai added to the swords' fearsome reputation.

The blade of a 16th century samurai katana

Ray skin and ornaments cover the **hilt** of a katana to aid grip

According to legend the samurai sword was developed by a swordsmith named Amakuni Yasutsuna. After seeing samurai return from battle with broken swords, he and his son locked themselves into their forge with the shattered weapons to discover what had gone wrong. They emerged one month later with an entirely new type of sword – the **katana**.

The blade is made from strips of different sorts of steel welded and hammered together. The back of the sword is coated in a **slurry** made from clay, ash, powdered stone, and water. The blade is then heated and plunged into cold water. The cutting edge cools very quickly which makes it hard and sharp. The edge covered by the slurry cools more slowly and so is more flexible, making it less likely to break.

The samurai carried two swords of different sizes, a pairing known as **daisho**. The swords were worn thrust through a sash around the samurai's waist. The pairing usually consisted of a katana and a **wakizashi**. The katana was the main fighting sword. It was slightly curved with a long two-handed hilt. The wakizashi was a little shorter with a single-handed hilt. It was used as a backup weapon for fighting indoors or for tasks such as slicing off the head of a dead enemy!

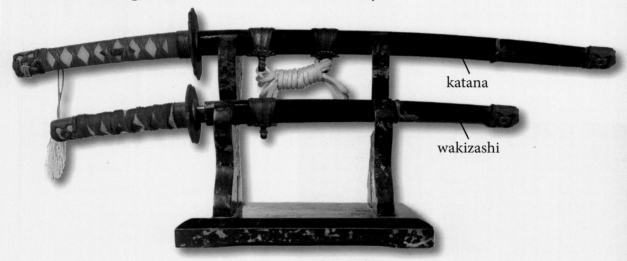

katana

wakizashi

THE DAISHO

In 1588, it was made illegal for anyone other than a samurai to wear the daisho swords. In 1629, a new law made it a duty for all samurai to wear the daisho when outside their home. Wearing the daisho became a visible sign of a samurai.

That's Fearless!

Samurai wore their katana with the blade facing upwards. This allowed them to draw the sword and be instantly ready to fight. A skilled swordsman was able to draw his katana and behead an enemy in less than a second.

Other Weapons

The samurai did not only use swords. They also used a wide variety of other edged weapons as well as weapons that could kill an enemy at a distance.

The early samurai were mounted warriors, skilled in the use of the long **yumi** bow. They trained for years to learn to shoot the bow from horseback, making them more skillful than the men who shot on foot.

The yumi was invented in about AD 700 and quickly became a standard weapon in Japan. It was made from layers of wood and bamboo, glued together and shaped into a double bend with the handle about a third of the way up. The bow is long and slender, making it light and powerful. The short lower section allows a man on horseback to switch the bow from one side of the horse to the other more easily.

The samurai used several weapons that were mounted on a long pole. The **naginata** had a curved blade. The **yari** had a long, straight blade. There were over a dozen types of yari that came in different lengths with blades that could be slim, wide, or have hooks to pull men from horses.

The **sasumata** was also mounted on a wooden pole. The head came in a variety of shapes and styles. They were often used by samurai when acting as policemen. Some had a mass of small hooks which would tangle in a suspect's clothing so he could be caught without injuring him. Another type had a U-shaped head that could be used to trap a suspect's neck against the ground to keep him from moving.

TANEGASHIMA

In 1543, a Portuguese ship ran ashore on the island of Tanegashima. To pay for the repairs the Portuguese gave the Lord of Tanegashima some guns. Local smiths began to make copies of the weapons and within ten years there were 300,000 "tanegashima" guns being used in Japan. Most samurai considered the gun to be a less honorable weapon than the sword and they were used mostly for hunting.

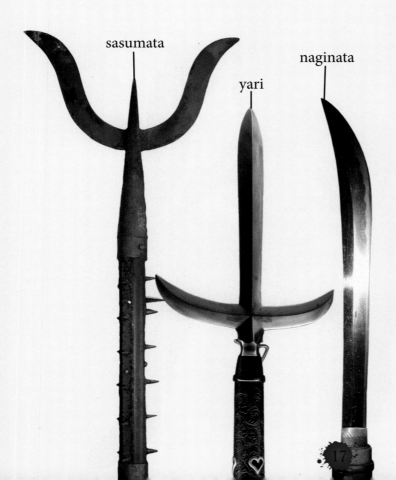

sasumata

yari

naginata

Samurai Armor

Samurai armor was designed to be as light and flexible as possible. Armor came in a variety of styles, depending on how it was to be used.

The early samurai wore armor made of small plates of metal or boiled leather covered with **lacquer** to make them waterproof. The plates were laced together with leather straps.

the helmet was usually made of three sheets of iron

curved sheets of iron or leather laced to the helmet protected the neck

arm armor had iron plates sewn inside cloth

square plates protected the shoulders

chest armor was usually made of iron

hinged plates hung from the front and back of the chest armor

iron plates laced together and suspended from the belt protected thighs

curved iron plates tied with silk lacing protected the shins

A samurai full suit of armor, known as an o-yoroi, was expensive and heavy. It was usually worn by horsemen.

Samurai identified each other by their armor. Each samurai clan had its own colors so even from a distance it was possible to tell which clan a samurai belonged to. Ordinary samurai had armor laced with leather, while commanders had silk lacing. The color of the lacing indicated the rank of the commander wearing it.

That's Fearless!

The samurai lord Maeda Toshiie loved colorful outfits. One spectacular suit of armor had metal plates gilded with a thin sheet of gold, then covered with clear lacquer so that the gold sparkled in the sun. The plates were then laced together with snow white silk ribbons. This outfit was worn over red silk clothing.

After the Japanese began using guns, a new type of armor called **tosei gusoku** was made. A breastplate made of a single sheet of thick iron was strong enough to withstand a bullet. Helmets were also made of this type of thick iron.

HIDDEN ARMOR

When not at war the samurai did not usually wear armor. However, leaders and rich samurai were often in danger from political rivals. They wore armor known as **kusari katabira**. This was a shirt made of iron mail which reached to the thighs and elbows. It could be worn hidden under normal clothing.

Samurai wearing kusari katabira and holding naginata

Sieges of fortified places were rare in samurai warfare. Earthquakes made building in stone difficult, so military buildings tended to be made of wood. When sieges did take place, they were major events.

Siege of Sanjo

In 1160, a nobleman named Minamoto no Yoshitomo captured Emperor Nijo and former Emperor Go-Shirakawa and set fire to the Sanjo palace. He forced Nijo to make him head of the government. Samurai clan leader Taira no Shigemori had been on a **pilgrimage**. He and his samurai rushed back to help. He smuggled Emperor Nijo out of the royal palace. Yoshitomo and his men barricaded the palace gates. Shigemori besieged the palace for 16 days, then marched his men away. It was a trap. As soon as Yoshitomo's men opened the gates, Shigemori and his best samurai attacked. Yoshitomo was killed and the emperor was restored to power.

The burning Sanjo Palace

Siege of Fushimi

In 1600, 4,000 men of the Toyotomi clan launched a surprise attack on the Tokugawa clan to capture Fushimi Castle. The castle was guarded by 2,000 men commanded by Torii Mototada. Knowing his Tokogawa lord needed nine days to gather his army, Mototada refused to surrender. On the tenth day of the siege the castle caught fire! Mototada led his surviving men in a charge against the enemy. They fought against overwhelming odds until only 10 of his men were left standing. Surrounded by his enemies, Mototada calmly sat down and killed himself to avoid capture, and so he kept his honor intact.

Fushimi Castle, Kyoto, rebuilt in 1964

SIEGE OF SACHEON

In 1598, the Chinese attacked Japan. The Chinese were supporting Korea which had been invaded by the Japanese. The Japanese were cornered in the fortress of Sacheon under samurai Shimazu Yoshihiro. His 7,000 men had to face 35,000 Chinese! The fortress was built on a rock that became an island at high tide. On the night of September 28 a wagon of gunpowder behind the Chinese lines suddenly exploded. The cascade of sparks set their tents and wagons on fire, and set off more gunpowder explosions. Seeing the confusion and panic in Chinese lines, Yoshihiro led an attack that sent the enemy running and ended the siege.

Samurai and Religion

The samurai believed that their honor was of enormous importance. They would commit ritual suicide rather than do anything dishonorable. Their code of honor, bushido, drew from several different religions.

The native religion of Japan is Shinto. This faith is still followed by around 80 percent of Japanese. Shinto has a wide number of gods and spirits, and emphasizes the importance of correct behavior and ritual practices. Shinto taught samurai that they must behave properly at all times.

Shinto temples usually have a torii gate at the entrance. This spectacular floating one is at Miyajima, Japan.

The faith of Buddhism began in India and came to Japan from China. The Buddhist belief that the soul is born and reborn endlessly made the samurai adopt a kinder approach to war. People were no longer killed needlessly, but only if it was necessary to win a battle. Torture, which had been common in Japan, was abandoned by about the year AD 900. Some samurai became Buddhist monks.

The Zen form of Buddhism teaches that a person can achieve spiritual peace and enlightenment through **meditation**. The samurai used Zen meditation to help them ignore their emotions and make decisions in a calm and rational way. Even in the heat of battle, samurai sought to remain calm while fighting for their lives.

CONFUCIUS

The Chinese faith of Confucianism is based on the teachings of the scholar Confucius. Confucius wanted to make society more fair and less violent. The samurai took from Confucianism the importance of being able to tell right from wrong. They also adopted his ideas for the need for a strictly organized society, and in particular the need to respect and obey one's lord.

A statue of Confucius

The Way of the Warrior

Bushido was the "way of the warrior," a samurai code that began in the 13th century. At first it was simply an idea of a few samurai, who wrote down some ideals that they thought younger samurai should try to reach. By the 18th century bushido was being taught formally at training academies.

The Glorious Death
All samurai aimed for a long life or a glorious death. Death had to be part of an important task that would become famous.

Loyalty
Loyalty to their lord was very important. Samurai Takeda Nobushige wrote: "In matters both great and small, one should not turn his back on his master's commands. No matter how unreasonably the master may treat a man . . . an underling does not pass judgments on a superior."

Courage
Bravery in battle was highly regarded by the samurai. Reckless behavior was not. Courage was necessary, but they must not put other lives at risk.

That's Fearless!
In the 17th century Nabeshima Naoshige stated: "It is shameful for any man to have not risked his life at least once in the line of duty, regardless of his rank."

General Akashi Gidayu preparing to kill himself

SEPPUKU

A samurai who had failed to follow bushido could redeem his honor by committing ritual suicide, or **seppuku**. This usually took place in front of invited guests. After eating a last meal and dressing in his finest clothes, the samurai would sit on a mat with his short sword in front of him. A samurai armed with a katana stood behind. The samurai read out his death poem that he had written. He then stabbed himself in the stomach. The samurai with the katana then struck, slicing off the man's head.

A painting of Oishi Yoshio, leader of the 47 ronin, committing seppuku

The Seven Virtues
According to historian Nitobe Inazo, the seven virtues of bushido were:
- righteousness
- courage
- benevolence
- respect
- sincerity
- honor
- loyalty

In 1600, samurai Torii Mototada volunteered to distract an enemy so that his lord and the main army could escape. He knew it meant his death. He wrote a letter to his son saying "That I should be able to lay down my life for the sake of my master's benevolence is an honor to my family and has been my most fervent desire for many years."

Women Samurai

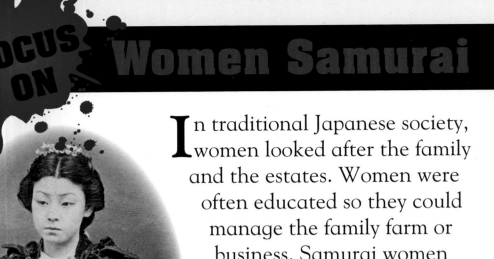

In traditional Japanese society, women looked after the family and the estates. Women were often educated so they could manage the family farm or business. Samurai women were trained to use weapons to defend their homes. A few women became famous samurai. They were called onna-bugeisha.

HANGAKU GOZEN

Hangaku came from a samurai family that had lost its lands after a war. As a girl she trained to use a bow on horseback and the naginata on foot. She raised an army of 3,000 soldiers to defend the fortress of Torisakayama for the **shogun** against an army of 10,000 from the Hojo clan. She held out for several days until she was hit by an arrow, fell ill, and was captured. She later married and settled down in Kai province.

Tomoe Gozon fell in love with the samurai Minamoto no Yoshinaka and followed him to war. When he was killed in battle, Tomoe wanted revenge. At the Battle of Awazu she killed Honda no Moroshige and Uchida Ieyoshi by slicing off their heads. She was defeated by Wada Yoshimori, who asked her to marry him! After his death Tomoe retired to become a nun.

The wife of Onodera Junai, one of the 47 ronin, preparing for jigai, the female version of seppuku

EMPRESS JINGU

When the Emperor Chuai died his wife Jingu ruled Japan until their baby son Ojin was old enough to inherit. Jingu was skilled with the bow and sword. She led a three-year invasion of Korea!

NAKANO TAKEKO

Nakano Takeko was talented with weapons at a young age. She became a martial arts instructor at Aizu and was working there when the Boshin War broke out. At the Battle of Aizu, Nakano used a naginata as she led a "women's army" of her best women pupils. She was shot in the chest when leading a charge and died soon after.

That's Fearless!

As Nakano Takeko lay dying she told her sister she did not want her head taken as a trophy by the enemy. Her sister cut off her head and buried it at a temple in Aizubange.

Surprise Attacks

Attacking from a hiding place was a favorite tactic. An enemy that is taken by surprise is an enemy that is not ready to fight.

Battle of Ishibashiyama

In 1180, the Minamoto clan of samurai was at war with the Taira government. Minamoto no Yoritomo camped in a forest with 300 men when a surprise night attack was launched by Oba Kagechika and 3,000 Taira samurai. The Minamoto fought a famous retreat that ended in a clearing dominated by a single large tree. When most of the Minamoto had been killed, Kagechika found that Yoritomo was not among the dead. He thought he must have escaped. In fact Yoritomo was hiding in the hollow tree trunk and escaped!

doves

Yoritomo

This sword hand guard shows Yoritomo hiding in the tree. When the Taira poked the tree two doves flew out, so they thought no one could be hiding there.

The Taira samurai chased Yoritomo, hoping to catch his small army before it could join allies from northern Japan. One night the Taira camped in a forest. Just after midnight the camp guards heard the sounds of many samurai running toward them through the forest. They raised the alarm and the Taira army fled. The noise had been caused by a flock of birds!

BATTLE OF OKEHAZAMA

In 1560, Imagawa Yoshimoto led an army of 25,000 men through Oda Nobunaga's land without permission. Insulted, Nobunaga decided to attack with only 2,000 samurai. He put 500 men on an easily defended hill to make Yoshimoto think that he was there. He then led his other 1,500 samurai through a forest to Yoshimoto's camp. It was a hot day and Yoshimoto's samurai had taken off their armor. Yoshimoto and his officers were eating a banquet in his command tent. When the Oda samurai charged out of the forest the unarmored enemy fled. Yoshimoto left his tent to tell his men to stop making so much noise, and was killed along with all his officers.

Yoshimoto is attacked as his army flees.

During the 16th century leading samurai began training their men in a series of **formations**. This meant that by simply giving a single order, an army would move into a complex formation to help fight different situations.

Key
- ● gunmen
- ▲ bowmen
- ■ spearmen
- ▮ samurai
- ◗ commander
- ◠ signals
- △ flags

GANKO "FLYING BIRDS"

In this formation samurai with edged weapons form a square in the center. Men with guns go to the front and rear. This standard start formation could be quickly transformed into another formation.

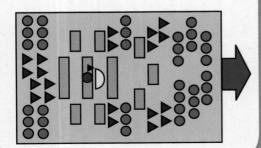

KAKUYOKU "WING OF THE CRANE"

Used when trying to surround an enemy with less men, the bows, spears and guns would soften up the enemy at the front, followed by one unit of samurai. Meanwhile a second unit of samurai, hidden behind the first, spreads out to surround the enemy.

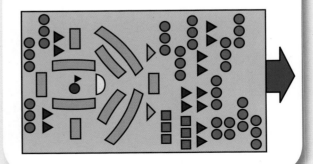

KOYAKU "OX YOKE"

In this defensive formation a small unit of samurai pushed some distance forward from the main army. This forced the enemy to attack before most of the samurai were committed to battle. The commander could then decide how to counterattack.

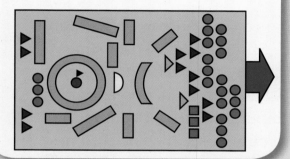

HOSHI "ARROW"

This triangular formation was designed to ensure a quick victory by smashing through an enemy formation. Bowmen went first and showered the enemy with arrows. Then the samurai charged to plunge through enemy ranks, and then fan out.

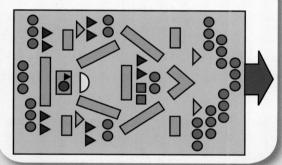

ENGETSU "CRESCENT MOON"

Designed for a fighting retreat when outnumbered, this formation has samurai armed with poles in a curved formation, backed by bowmen and gunmen. The units take it in turns to march back, covered by the others.

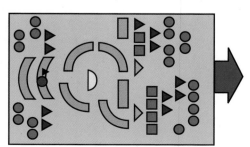

SAKU "KEYHOLE"

This formation has a circle of samurai with two wings of bowmen and gunmen at the front. A charging enemy would be cut down before reaching the defensive circle.

Unexpected Tactics

Samurai were trained to use weapons and tactics in the most effective ways, but some samurai broke the rules and used unexpected tactics to achieve success.

Battle of Ichi-no-Tani

A Taira army of 5,000 men was camped on a narrow strip of land between the mountains and the sea. Minamoto no Yoshitsune divided his army of 3,000 men into three columns for an attack.

One column marched over the mountains to get behind the Taira. A second sneaked up the slopes above the Taira. The third stayed with Yoshitsune. A drum signaled all three columns to attack at once. The Taira ran to their ships and fled.

That's Fearless!

The death of the young prince Taira no Atsumori in single combat with Kumagai Naozane at the Battle of Ichi-no-Tani became legendary. Atsumori was a talented flute player and admired by Naozane. Naozane did not recognize Atsumori in his armor until after his death. Noazane was so upset by what he had done that he became a monk.

Battle of Uji

A civil war erupted within the Minamoto clan. Minamoto no Yoshitsune left Kyoto with Emperor Go-Shirakawa as a hostage. He destroyed the only bridge over the Uji River, then waited on the far side for his cousin Minamoto no Yoshinaka who was in pursuit. Yoshinaka saw the demolished bridge, and appeared to retreat. In fact he knew a nearby ford that could be used by mounted men. Yoshinaka led his cavalry over the ford and defeated Yoshitsune.

Battle of Anegawa

Oda Nobunaga and his allies were besieging the castles of the Azai and Asakura clans. They were attacked by both clans storming across the Ane River. Nobunaga was forced to withdraw men from the siege, which allowed Asakura forces from the castle to join the fighting in the river. Nobunaga was forced back, but his ally Tokugawa Ieyasu arrived to help. They won and Nobunaga's victory gave him control of the Azai clan.

SCARING THE HORSES

Oda Nobunaga led an army to break the siege of his castle at Nagashino. He arrived to find the Takeda clan blocking his path with 15,000 men. The Takeda clan had won many battles with their fierce cavalry charges. Nobunaga ordered his men to build several small circular wooden barriers and stand behind them. When the Takeda charged, their horses shied away from the barriers and backed into open space. Nobunaga's infantry opened fire, shooting down the disorganized cavalry. The Takeda forces fled.

Decisive Battles

For centuries the samurai clans fought each other to decide which would lead the government of Japan. Most battles led only to more fighting, but a few battles were so decisive that they settled the question for generations.

BATTLE OF SEKIGAHARA

After years of war between rival samurai clans, Japan was split between two great alliances. One was led by Toyotomi Hideyori, the other by Tokugawa Ieyasu. In 1600, Hideyori went with an army of 120,000 men to attack Ieyasu's 80,000 men at Sekigahara. Unknown to Hideyori, many of his allies had been persuaded by Ieyasu to change sides, or not fight at all. When they gave the order to advance, several of his clan commanders refused. One even sent back a message that he was too busy eating his breakfast! Ieyasu counterattacked. Realizing that they had been betrayed, the men fled. The victory gave power to Ieyasu, who became shogun three years later.

Battle of Dan-no-ura

This naval battle marked the end of Taira power in Japan. Emperor Antoku and the Taira fleet of 500 ships was attacked by 800 Minamoto ships in the straits of Dan-no-ura. At first archers on both sides shot arrows at the other's ships. As the ships got closer samurai began boarding enemy ships to fight hand-to-hand. The tide changed and swept the ships into the narrow straits. The emperor's ship tried to escape, but one of his own samurai pointed the ship out to the Minamoto. The Minamoto closed in. A Taira samurai killed the emperor rather than see him captured. Several Taira samurai then committed suicide out of shame and the rest fled.

BATTLE OF TOBA–FUSHIMI

In January 1868, Japan was in chaos as Emperor Meiji tried to modernize government against the wishes of the powerful Tokugawa clan. Tokugawa Yoshinobu and 15,000 men took a letter of protest to the emperor in Kyoto. They met a barricade and gunfire at the bridge at Toba. After three days of fighting Yoshinobu fled to his fortress at Edo.

BATTLE OF UENO

In July 1868, the Tokugawa's outpost at Ueno was attacked by Emperor Meiji's supporters led by Omura Masujiro. The fighting became a major battle as more forces joined. Masujiro used modern weapons, making the traditional samurai weapons almost useless. After heavy losses, the Tokugawa fled and the fortress at Edo was taken.

Supreme Samurai

All samurai aimed to live their lives according to the code of bushido, but some samurai proved to be more skilled and honorable than any others.

Minamoto no Yoritomo

Leader of the Minamoto clan of samurai, Yoritomo fought a long series of wars against other clans and the imperial court between 1170 and 1185. Yoritomo forced Emperor Go-Toba to give him the title of shogun, the supreme military commander. He then stripped power from the emperor and nobles, and handed power to the samurai who had supported him.

HASEKURA TSUNENAGA

After serving in wars against Korea and as a government official, Tsunenaga was chosen by shogun Tokugawa Hidetada to be the first Japanese ambassador to go to Europe. Hidetada wanted to learn about European weapons, religion, and to establish trade. Hidetada, a guard of samurai, plus merchants and servants went on the long overseas journey to Spain, then to Rome and France.

Hasekura's portrait painted during his time in Rome

KUSUNOKI MASASHIGE

Generations of samurai honored Masashige as the most loyal samurai who ever lived. In 1331 he joined the forces loyal to Emperor Go-Daigo as he tried to take power away from the Shogun Morinaga. At first they were successful, largely due to Masashige's clever tactics, but in 1336 the shogun forces attacked Kyoto. Masashige suggested a battle plan, but Go-Daigo refused to leave his capital and ordered Masashige to attack the enemy. Knowing to obey the order would mean his death, Masashige wrote a death poem and sent it to his son. He then declared "I wish I had seven lives to give for my emperor" and rode to his death.

Yamaoka Tesshu

Tesshu was born in 1836 and he was one of the last samurai. When he was only nine years old he was already highly skilled with the katana sword. When he finished his training, he became the head of a sword training school. In 1868 Tesshu became head bodyguard to the shogun. He played a key role in getting agreements between the modernizers and traditionalists. When he realized that he was dying of cancer he wrote a death poem, sat on a mat, closed his eyes, and allowed death to creep over him.

In 1853, a fleet of American warships invaded Japanese waters and ended the Japanese policy of isolation. Realizing other nations had more powerful armies and richer societies, the Japanese embarked on a massive modernization program.

In the 1630s the Japanese government had become worried about foreign influences. In 1635, the government introduced "sakoku," a policy of isolation. It was illegal for any foreigner to enter Japan or for anyone to leave. Christianity was banned. Trade with foreigners was possible only on the small island of Dejima, and only under strict government control.

AN UNFAIR TREATY

America forced Japan to sign a treaty in 1854. The treaty allowed America to decide what they could sell in Japan, what taxes they would pay, and which laws Americans in Japan would obey. Soon Britain, France, and other countries imposed similar treaties. Many people in Japan feared that they were about to be invaded and conquered.

Many Japanese believed the only way to save Japan from invasion was to remove the old system and to modernize. Led by senior samurai such as Saigo Takamori and Kido Takayoshi, they introduced European-style industry and trade. They stripped the shogun of power and restored power to the Emperor Meiji, who supported the reformers.

Samurai who were unhappy at the changes launched a **rebellion** which led to the Boshin War in 1868. After more than a year of fighting the rebellion was crushed.

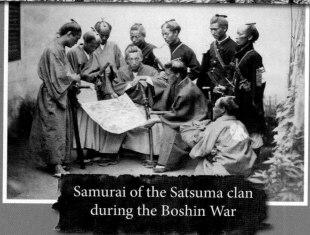

Samurai of the Satsuma clan during the Boshin War

Under the new reforms the privileges, rights, and duties of the samurai were abolished. Because the samurai were the best educated people in Japan, they took government jobs, founded businesses, and became political leaders. Some of their descendants remain important to this day.

That's Fearless!

During the Boshin War, samurai Hijikata Toshizo was trapped by government forces. He mounted his horse, drew his katana sword and charged the army. After he was killed a poem was found which read: "Though my body may decay on the island of Ezo, My spirit guards my lord in the east."

Samurai Timeline

For more than a thousand years the samurai dominated Japan. The samurai developed from servants to masters, from killers to educated artists.

- **700 Samurai Swords**
  The date when swordsmith Amakuni Yasutsuna was believed to have developed the techniques for making samurai swords.

- **797 Early Bushido**
  The book *Shoku Nihongi* makes the earliest reference to bushido, the way of the warrior.

700 ● ● ● ● 800

- **702 Taiho Code**
  The Taiho Code introduced a military system where adult men could choose to serve in the army and provide their own weapons in return for not paying any taxes on their land. Some of these men were referred to as "samurai."

- **c.800 Samurai**
  Emperor Kammu disbands the national army and relies on soldiers recruited by his nobles. The samurai soldiers start to organize themselves into clans under their own commanders.

c.980 Swordsmithing

Approximate date when swordsmithing techniques producing samurai swords become widespread.

c.1180 Bushido

The book *Heike Monogatari* gives a description of the ideal samurai as following bushido and skilled in both fighting and the arts.

1180 Genpei War

The outbreak of the five-year Genpei War between the Taira and Minamoto clans.

900

1000

1185 Minamoto no Yoritomo

Samurai leader Minamoto no Yoritomo defeats the Taira and becomes shogun. He promotes samurai into government positions. This establishes the samurai class as the real rulers of Japan.

1100

1200

c.1280 Swordsmith Masamune

The swordsmith Masamune perfects the art of making the perfect samurai sword. He is thought to have made only 61 swords, of which only three survive today.

A statue of Minamoto samurai Minamoto no Yoshitsune

c.1400 Katana Swords

The katana sword with its long, slightly curved blade is developed.

a katana

c.1490 Foot Soldiers

Japanese samurai clans start to recruit large numbers of poorly trained non-samurai foot soldiers. The samurai increasingly become elite warriors and officers rather than ordinary fighting men.

c.1480 Power Struggle

The shogunate begins to lose power as samurai clan leaders and lords gain powers and military might. Small-scale raids and wars between the samurai clans become increasingly common in the decades that follow.

1500

1400

1543 Guns

The crew of a stranded Portuguese ship gives two matchlocks to the local samurai lord. The Japanese start to produce guns.

c.1450 Short Swords

The short wakizashi sword is developed as a secondary weapon for samurai.

1588 Wearing the Daisho

It is made illegal for anyone other than a samurai to wear the daisho, the combination of the katana and wakizashi swords.

A samurai wearing the daisho

- **1600 Battle of Sekigahara**
The Battle of Sekigahara leads to the establishment of the Tokugawa Shogunate and centuries of peace within Japan. The generations of samurai that follow continue to train with weapons, but also spend their time as land owners or government officials instead of warriors.

Emperor Meiji

1600

1700

- **1867**
A group of samurai forces the abolition of the shogunate and restores power to the Emperor Meiji. They aim to modernize Japan, while respecting ancient traditions.

- **1853 American Warships**
A fleet of American warships forces its way into Edo harbor and forces the Japanese government to open its borders to trade and contact with the outside world.

1800

1900

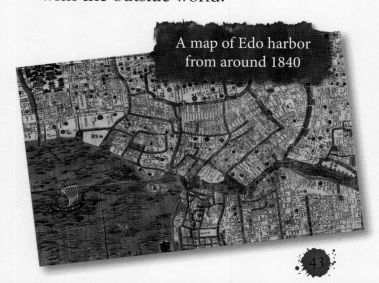
A map of Edo harbor from around 1840

- **1876 The End of the Samurai**
Wearing the daisho in public is made illegal, ending the samurai's exclusive right to carry weapons. The legal status of the samurai is abolished two years later.

What Do You Know?

Can you answer these questions about the Samurai?

1. What did the word "saburai" originally mean?

2. At what age did boys start to train with metal weapons?

3. How long could the tea ceremony, or "Way of Tea," take?

4. In what year was the legal status of samurai abolished?

5. Which artistic skill was most highly regarded by samurai?

6. What type of garden did samurai use to aid contemplation?

7. What is a katana?

8. Why did samurai paint their armor with different colors of lacquer?

9. What was a ronin?

10. What is Shinto?

Answers on page 48

Further Information

Books

Macdonald, Fiona. *Avoid Being a Samurai!* Brighton, UK: Salariya, 2009.

Stowell, Louie. *Samurai.* Oxford, UK: Usborne Publishing, 2007.

Turnbull, Stephen. *Samurai: The Japanese Warrior's (Unofficial) Manual.* London, UK: Thames & Hudson, 2012.

Turnbull, Stephen. *Samurai Women 1184-1877.* Oxford, UK: Osprey, 2010.

Websites

Encyclopedia.com entry
http://www.encyclopedia.com/topic/samurai.aspx

Kids Web Japan, information on Japan, the Samurai, and shoguns
http://web-japan.org/kidsweb/explore/history/
http://web-japan.org/kidsweb/explore/history/q8.html

Glossary

abolished When a behavior or activity that was once common stops happening due to a change in the law it has been abolished.

bunbo ryodo A phrase used to describe an action in which military skill was combined with literary activity to produce a masterpiece. The phrase means "the pen and sword in one accord."

bushido "The way of the warrior," the code of honor that all samurai were expected to follow.

ceremonial A person or object that takes part in an action that has symbolic meaning rather than real importance.

daisho The pair of swords worn by a samurai in his waist sash.

descendants A person's children, grandchildren, and future generations are that person's descendants.

durability The ability to last a long time.

formations Groups of soldiers who stand together in such a way that they are more effective.

hilt The handle of a sword. Samurai swords often had hilts that featured precious materials or exquisite works of art.

kabukimono Ronin who earn a living through crime.

katana The long, curved sword traditionally carried by samurai.

kusari katabira A shirt made of chain mail armor.

lacquer A type of varnish that dries to an extremely hard, shiny, and waterproof finish.

meditation An activity where a person trains his mind to concentrate while blocking out distractions.

naginata An edged blade weapon on a wooden pole.

piety A virtue that involves a person dedicating their lives to religious study or to behaving in a particular way that is thought to be approved of by a god or gods.

pilgrimage A journey that involves visiting sacred places where the person usually takes part in religious ceremonies.

rebellion To disobey a person in authority; often this involves trying to replace that person with somebody else.

rural Belonging to or coming from the countryside as opposed to the town.

sasumata A weapon mounted on a pole used to catch criminals without killing them.

seppuku Suicide following a ritual pattern by which a disgraced samurai could regain his honor.

shogun Originally the head of the army, later the head of the government.

slurry A mix of powders turned into a gloopy paste by being mixed with water or oil.

tosei gusoku A type of armor made from iron plates, first produced in Japan about the year 1500.

uruwashii A samurai who is not only highly skilled as a warrior but also as an artist or writer.

wakizashi The shorter sword traditionally carried by samurai.

yari A spear with a straight blade.

yumi A type of bow made from laminated layers of wood and bamboo.

Index

Answers to Quiz

1. a person who serves a nobleman
2. nine years of age
3. around four hours
4. 1878
5. writing poetry
6. a stone garden
7. the long, curved sword used as the principal weapon of samurai
8. so that other samurai could tell to which clan they belonged
9. samurai who did not serve a lord
10. Japanese religion that honors different gods and spirits